USEFUL INFORMATION

The recipes in this book are all thoroughly tested,
using standard metric measuring cups and spoons.
All cup and spoon measurements are level.
We have used eggs with an average weight of 60 g each
in all recipes.

WEIGHTS AND MEASURES

In this book, metric measures and their imperial equivalents have been rounded out to the nearest figure that is easy to use. Different charts from different authorities vary slightly; the following are the measures we have used consistently throughout our recipes.

OVEN TEMPERATURE CHART

	°C	°F
Very slow	120	250
Slow	150	300
Mod. slow	160	325
Moderate	180	350
Mod. hot	210 (190 gas)	425
Hot	240 (200 gas)	475
Very hot	260 (230 gas)	525

LENGTH

Metric	Imperial
5 mm	¼ in
1 cm	½ in
2 cm	¾ in
2½ cm	1 in
5 cm	2 in
8 cm	3 in
10 cm	4 in
12 cm	5 in
15 cm	6 in
20 cm	8 in
25 cm	10 in
30 cm	12 in
46 cm	18 in
50 cm	20 in
61 cm	24 in

CUP AND SPOON MEASURES

A basic metric cup set consists of 1 cup, ½ cup, ⅓ cup and ¼ cup sizes.

The basic spoon set comprises 1 tablespoon, 1 teaspoon, ½ teaspoon and ¼ teaspoon.

1 cup	250 ml (8 fl oz)
½ cup	125 ml (4 fl oz)
⅓ cup (4 tablespoons)	80 ml (2½ fl oz)
¼ cup (3 tablespoons)	60 ml (2 fl oz)
1 tablespoon	20 ml
1 teaspoon	5 ml
½ teaspoon	2.5 ml
¼ teaspoon	1.25 ml

LIQUIDS

Metric	Imperial
30 ml	1 fl oz
60 ml	2 fl oz
100 ml	3½ fl oz
125 ml	4 fl oz (½ cup)
155 ml	5 fl oz
170 ml	5½ fl oz (⅔ cup)
200 ml	6½ fl oz
250 ml	8 fl oz (1 cup)
300 ml	9½ fl oz
375 ml	12 fl oz
410 ml	13 fl oz
470 ml	15 fl oz
500 ml	16 fl oz (2 cups)
600 ml	1 pt (20 fl oz)
750 ml	1 pt 5 fl oz (3 cups)
1 litre (1000 ml)	1 pt 12 fl oz (4 cups)

DRY INGREDIENTS

Metric	Imperial
15 g	½ oz
30 g	1 oz
45 g	1½ oz
60 g	2 oz
75 g	2½ oz
100 g	3½ oz
125 g	4 oz
155 g	5 oz
185 g	6 oz
200 g	6½ oz
250 g	8 oz
300 g	9½ oz
350 g	11 oz
375 g	12 oz
400 g	12½ oz
425 g	13½ oz
440 g	14 oz
470 g	15 oz
500 g	1 lb (16 oz)
750 g	1 lb 8 oz
1 kg (1000 g)	2 lb

best of
KiDS'
COOKING

MURDOCH BOOKS®

Sydney • London • Vancouver

CONTENTS

Something yummy for monster and me

HAMBURGER WITH THE LOT

Makes 4

500 g hamburger mince
110 g packet hamburger
  seasoning mix
¼ cup oil
1 large onion,
  sliced into rings
4 rashers bacon
4 eggs

4 hamburger buns
4 slices Cheddar cheese
1 cup shredded lettuce
1 medium tomato, sliced
8 slices beetroot, well
  drained
4 pineapple rings
⅓ cup tomato sauce

Wash lettuce well to get rid of dirt and any bugs that may be hiding among the leaves. Wash under running water and then dry with paper towels.

1. Mix mince and seasoning in a bowl. Shape into 4 patties.

2. Heat oil in a big, heavy pan. Fry patties 3 minutes, turn and cook other side 3 minutes.

3. Drain on paper towels, cover and keep warm.

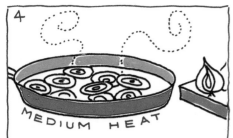

4. Fry onions until golden; drain on paper towels.

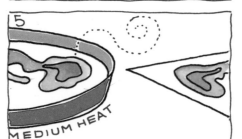

5. Fry bacon until crisp; drain on paper towels.

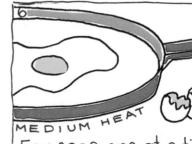

6. Fry eggs one at a time; keep warm.

7. Cut open buns. Toast until golden.

8. Lay everything on bun bottoms. Top with sauce, put top on and serve.

HOT BEAN DOGS

Makes 4

4 continental frankfurts
4 hot dog rolls
120 g butter
225 g can baked beans in tomato sauce
4 tablespoons coarsely grated Cheddar cheese
4 tablespoons sweet mustard

1. Cut 5 slits into each frankfurt.

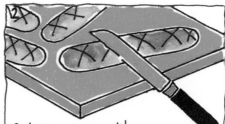

2. Cut 5 more slits across the first to make a pattern.

3. Put franks under hot grill. When one side is brown, turn and cook the other side.

4. Split rolls in half and spread with butter.

5. Put rolls on plates. Spoon baked beans on rolls.

6. Sprinkle with cheese.

7. Put hot frankfurt on top of cheese. (Use tongs.)

8. Top with a spoon of mustard and serve.

FANCY FISH FINGERS

Serves 4

¹⁄₃ cup tomato relish
12 fish fingers
3 slices processed cheese
4 rashers bacon

1 Turn oven to 200°c (400°F).

2 Spread relish on one side of each fish finger.

3 Cut each cheese slice into 4 strips.

4 Lay a slice over relish.

5 Cut bacon into long thin strips.

6 Wrap bacon around each finger.

7 Place fingers on an oven tray (you don't need to grease the tray).

8 Bake 10 minutes. Serve hot.

Serves 4

1 x 310 g can whole kernel corn
2 eggs
sprinkle of salt and pepper
½ cup plain flour
1 teaspoon baking powder
¼ cup grated cheese
25 g butter
2 tablespoons oil

1

Drain corn. Discard liquid.

2

Put eggs, salt + pepper in a bowl. Beat well.

3

Add flour + baking powder. Whisk until smooth.

4

Add drained corn and grated cheese. Stir.

5

MEDIUM HEAT

Put butter + oil in frypan. Heat until bubbly.

6

MEDIUM HEAT

Drop spoonsful of the mixture in.

7

When golden, turn over and cook other side.

8

Drain on absorbent paper and serve.

SCHNITZEL SANDWICH

Makes 2

¼ cup oil
1 onion, sliced
2 Vienna schnitzels
4 thick slices bread,
   lightly toasted
2 eggs
2 tablespoons barbecue
   sauce
1 tomato, sliced

Heat half the oil in a big, heavy fry pan.

Fry onions until brown. Take out of pan, drain on absorbent paper. Keep warm.

Pour the rest of the oil into the fry pan.

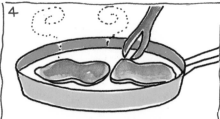

Cook schnitzels for 2 minutes. Turn over and cook the other side for 2 minutes.

Put schnitzels on toast. Top with onions.

Fry eggs. Put the cooked eggs on top of the onions.

Pour on sauce and put tomato on top.

Top with toast and serve hot.

CHICKEN FILLET BURGERS

Makes 2

1 egg, lightly beaten
¼ cup cornflour
1 cup cornflake crumbs
2 tablespoons desiccated
   coconut
2 chicken breast fillets
2 tablespoons oil
2 hamburger buns

1 banana, sliced diagonally
½ cup shredded lettuce
½ cup grated carrot
¼ cup alfalfa sprouts
¼ cup fruit chutney
⅓ cup grated Cheddar
   cheese

Burgers can be a really healthy, energy-giving meal – use lean minced meat, chicken or fish, be generous with the salad ingredients and use wholemeal buns.

1 Put egg and cornflour in a small bowl. Mix until smooth.

2 Put cornflake crumbs and coconut on a flat plate.

3 Dip chicken into egg mixture and then roll in crumbs.

4 Heat oil in a big, heavy pan.

5 Add chicken and cook 3 minutes. Turn and cook other side 3 minutes until golden.

6 Take out and put on paper towels to drain.

7 Open up buns. Put banana, lettuce, carrot and alfalfa on bottom halves.

8 Add chicken, chutney and grated cheese. Put top on. Serve immediately.

CHOCANANA MUFFINS

Makes 12

1 small ripe banana
1 cup white self-raising
　flour
½ cup wholemeal
　self-raising flour
⅔ cup sugar
½ cup choc bits
1 egg, lightly beaten
⅔ cup milk
¼ cup oil

1

Turn oven to 180°c (350°F).

2

Brush a 12-hole muffin pan with a little oil.

3

Mash banana in a large bowl.

4

Sift flour into the bowl (add the husks left in the sifter).

5

Put in sugar, choc bits, egg, milk and oil.

6

Stir with a fork until well mixed.

7

Spoon mixture into muffin pan. Fill the holes ⅔ full.

Yummy hot muffins make a great snack. Drink a glass of milk or soy milk with a Chocanana Muffin and you'll be absolutely bursting with energy.

8

Bake for 20 minutes or until golden. Turn onto a rack to cool.

CINNAMON TOAST

Serves 6

6 tablespoons caster sugar
2 tablespoons cinnamon
6 thick slices bread
softened butter

1
Put the sugar into a small jar or cup.

2
Add the cinnamon and stir until mixed.

3
Put the bread in toaster.

4
Toast it until golden.

5
Butter toast immediately.

6
Sprinkle cinnamon and sugar evenly over.

7
Slice the toast + serve.

8
Put lid on jar and use any leftover cinnamon + sugar any time.

HAM AND PINEAPPLE

Serves 4

4 canned pineapple rings
  in pineapple juice
2 tablespoons brown sugar
4 ham steaks (about 1 cm
  thick)
75 g butter

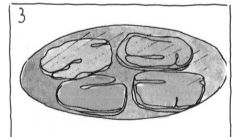

1

Drain pineapple rings.
Save ½ cup of the juice.

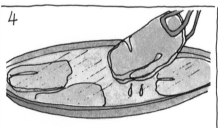

2

Put juice + brown sugar
in a large flat dish.

3

Put steaks in. Put in fridge.
Leave in fridge 3 hours.

4

Turn steaks over every
hour.

5

Heat butter in large frying
pan. Drain the ham.

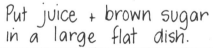

6

Fry ham till golden.
Turn steaks often.

7

Fry pineapple for a few
minutes at the end.

8

Serve with a salad.
Serves 4 people.

CHICKEN POCKETS

Makes 2

2 oval pocket breads
2 tablespoons mayonnaise
3 large lettuce leaves
2 tablespoons corn relish
10 chicken nuggets

1. Carefully split pocket breads open.

2. Put bread on serving plates.

3. Spread mayonnaise on inside of bread.

4. Chop lettuce thinly.

5. Fill bread pockets with lettuce. Spoon relish over.

6. Grill chicken nuggets 3 minutes.

7. Turn nuggets; cook 3 minutes more.

8. Put cooked nuggets into pockets. Serve hot.

HAM AND CHEESE PUFFS

Makes 2

1 sheet ready-rolled puff pastry
2 slices sandwich ham
2 slices tasty cheese

1 Turn oven to 180°c (350°F).

2 Put pastry on large cutting board. Cut into 4 squares.

3 Put the slices of ham on 2 pieces of pastry.

4 Top the ham with the cheese slices.

5 Put the plain pastry on top. Press edges together.

6 Trim around edges with a pastry wheel.

7 Put on a baking tray. Bake for 12 minutes.

8 Cut in half to serve.

GARLIC TOAST

Serves 4

25 g butter
½ teaspoon garlic salt
6 thin slices wholegrain
   bread

Turn oven to 150°C (300°F)

LOW HEAT

Melt the butter.

Mix in the garlic.

Spread it on each
piece of bread.

Cut each piece of bread
into 3 strips.

Put (butter side up) on to
an oven sheet.

Bake for 30 minutes.

Serve hot with soup.

NACHOS

Serves 2

½ cup three bean mix
1 cup corn chips
¼ cup taco sauce
¼ cup chopped avocado
¼ cup grated mozzarella
    cheese
1 tablespoon sour cream

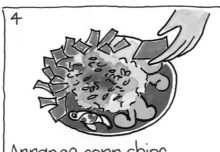

1

Turn oven to 180°C (350°F).

2

Put beans in a bowl. Mash with a fork.

3

Spoon beans into the centre of 2 ovenproof dishes.

4

Arrange corn chips around the beans.

5

Pour taco sauce on the beans.

6

Put avocado on top of sauce.

7

Sprinkle the grated cheese over.

8

Bake for 10 minutes. Serve topped with a spoonful of sour cream.

APPLE MUFFINS

Makes about 12

1 cup wholemeal
  self-raising flour
½ cup brown sugar
½ cup oat bran
½ teaspoon cinnamon
¼ cup chopped pecans
2 large green apples

1 egg
⅔ cup milk
60 g butter, melted

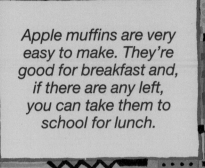
Apple muffins are very easy to make. They're good for breakfast and, if there are any left, you can take them to school for lunch.

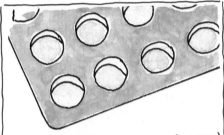

1. Turn oven to 220°C (425°F) Grease 12 muffin pans.

2. Sift flour into a bowl. Add sugar, oat bran, cinnamon + pecans.

3. Peel, then grate the apples. Stir them into the bowl.

4. Mix egg, milk and melted butter in a jug.

5. Add to bowl all at once. Stir with a fork.

6. Stir until just mixed. It is supposed to look lumpy.

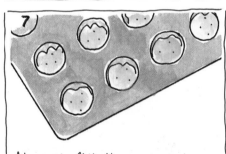

7. Almost fill the pans with the batter.

8. Bake 15–20 minutes or until golden

Serve warm with butter + jam if you like

19

TASTY TUNA TRIANGLES

Makes 12 triangles

170 g can sandwich tuna
130 g can creamed corn
1 tablespoon chopped
   parsley leaves
1 egg
6 slices white bread
⅓ cup oil

1
Pour tuna and corn into a mixing bowl.

2
Add the chopped parsley and egg. Mix well.

3
Cut crusts off bread.

4
Spread mixture on bread slices.

5
Cut slices into triangles.

6
Heat the oil in a fry pan. When it's hot, put in a few triangles.

7
When they are golden lift out with a spatula and put on paper to drain.

8
Cook the rest of the triangles and drain on paper.

COFFEE FLOAT

Serves 6

2 tablespoons instant coffee
  powder
2 tablespoons sugar
³/₄ cup hot water
1 teaspoon vanilla essence
4 cups cold milk
6 scoops vanilla ice-cream
cocoa powder, to sprinkle

1

Dissolve coffee and sugar in the hot water.

2

Pour into a bowl. Add the vanilla essence and milk.

3

Stir it all well.

4

Chill in the fridge until it's very cold.

5

Whisk until it's foamy.

6

Put a scoop of ice-cream into 6 tall glasses.

7

Fill each glass with mixture.

8

Sprinkle with a little cocoa powder. Pop in a straw and serve.

BANANA MILKSHAKE

Serves 3

1½ cups milk
1 medium-sized banana
1 tablespoon honey
1 egg
2 tablespoons banana-
   flavoured yoghurt
2 scoops vanilla ice-cream
2 ice cubes

1

Pour milk into blender.

2

Peel the banana.

3

Chop up the banana.
Add it to the blender.

4

Add the honey, egg
and banana yoghurt.

5

Add ice cream + ice.

6

Put lid on blender.
Blend well until smooth.

7

Pour it into 3 glasses.

8

Pop in straws + serve.

FRUIT PUNCH

Serves 10

1.25 L canned orange juice
425 g can fruit salad
1 orange
1 lemon
750 mL bottle of lemonade
   (chilled)

1. Pour the can of juice into a large bowl or jug.

2. Add the whole can of fruit salad.

3. Squeeze juice from orange

4. Pour it into bowl.

5. Squeeze juice from lemon Add it to bowl.

6. Put in the fridge until it's really cold.

7. Just before serving, add the lemonade.

8. Stir it and then serve it.

PIZZA SUPREME

Serves 4

1 large pizza base
½ cup bottled spaghetti
   sauce
2 cups grated mozzarella
   cheese
1 onion
125 g button mushrooms
½ medium green capsicum
200 g can peeled prawns,
   drained
100 g cabanossi
100 g pepperoni
12 black olives, pitted

1  Turn oven to 200°c (400°F).	2 Grease pizza tray. Put pizza base on tray.	3 Spread with spaghetti sauce and ½ the cheese.
4  Cut onion, mushrooms and capsicum (throw away seeds) into thin slices.	5  Arrange vegetables on pizza.	6  Sprinkle prawns and remaining cheese over.
7 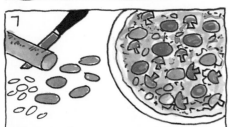 Slice cabanossi and pepperoni. Arrange on pizza with olives.	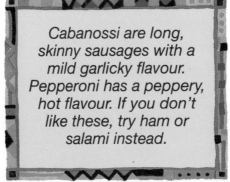 *Cabanossi are long, skinny sausages with a mild garlicky flavour. Pepperoni has a peppery, hot flavour. If you don't like these, try ham or salami instead.*	8  Bake 25 minutes. Serve hot.

BIG PIZZA

Serves 4

2 cups self-raising flour
¼ teaspoon salt
30 g butter
1 cup milk
1 tablespoon oil
¼ cup tomato sauce

2 cups grated Cheddar
 cheese
1 tomato, thinly sliced
1 cup well drained
 pineapple pieces
1 cup finely chopped ham
 (or salami)

If you don't have time to make the dough for pizza, you can buy frozen pizza bases from the supermarket.

1

Turn oven to 220°C (425°F). Get out a large oven tray.

2

Sift flour + salt into bowl. Chop up butter and add.

3

With fingers, rub in butter until blended in.

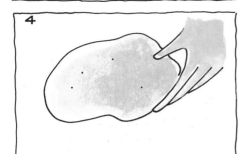

4

Add milk (more if needed) and knead + mix to a soft dough.

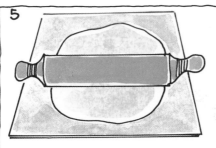

5

Roll it out on the baking tray until 34 cm in diameter

6

Brush dough with oil then the tomato sauce.

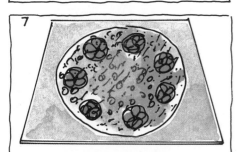

7

Sprinkle cheese over, arrange tomato slices on top.

8

Spread pineapple and ham evenly over.

Bake 20-25 minutes or until cooked.

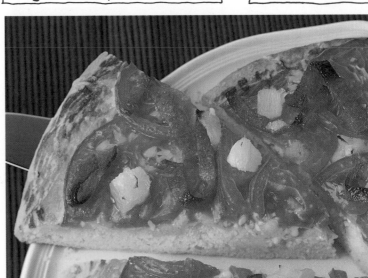

PINEAPPLE PAN PIZZA

Serves 2

2 teaspoons oil
1 Lebanese bread
2 tablespoons tomato
  paste
½ teaspoon dried oregano
  leaves

100 g Cheddar cheese
125 g sliced ham
60 g pepperoni
2 canned pineapple rings,
  drained

This is a really quick pizza recipe, and you don't have to heat up the oven – a good idea on hot summer days.

1 Grease a big non-stick pan with the oil.

2 Spread bread with tomato paste. Sprinkle on oregano.

3 Grate cheese coarsely. Sprinkle over bread.

4 Put bread in pan.

5 Cut ham and pepperoni into thin strips.

6 Arrange over bread.

7 Chop pineapple rings and arrange over pizza.

8 Cover pizza and cook gently for 8 minutes.

LOW HEAT

28

MEATY PIZZA WEDGES

Makes 40

2 cups self-raising flour
100 g butter, chopped
½ cup buttermilk
2 tablespoons tomato paste
1 stick cabanossi, thinly
   sliced
1 small onion, thinly sliced
10 cherry tomatoes, thinly
   sliced
6 cheese slices, cut into
   3 cm rounds

1 Turn oven to 180°c. Line two baking trays with foil then grease the foil.

2  Sift flour into a bowl. Use your fingertips to rub the flour + butter together until they look like breadcrumbs

3  Use a kitchen knife to stir in the buttermilk. Mix together until it makes a soft dough.

4  Sprinkle a little flour on a board and knead the dough on it.

5 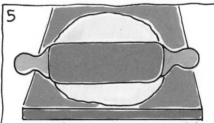 Roll out the dough until it is quite thin (about 3 mm).

6  Cut out circles of dough using a 5cm cutter. (Dip the cutter in flour first to stop the dough sticking.)

7 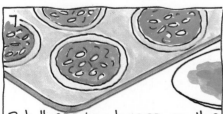 Put the pizza bases on the baking trays. Spread them with tomato paste then put cabanossi, onion + tomato on.

8  Put a slice of cheese on top of each pizza + bake for 10 minutes until crisp.

You can put almost anything on top of pizzas. Try chopped ham and pineapple. Or pepperoni, if you're feeling brave!

CORNY CHICKEN CANNELLONI

Serves 4

250 g packet frozen
chopped leaf spinach

1 small onion, finely chopped

30 g butter

250 g chicken mince

130 g can corn kernels,
drained

130 g can diced capsicum,
drained

2 tablespoons dried
breadcrumbs

1 egg, lightly beaten

120 g packet instant
cannelloni shells

250 ml bottled spaghetti
sauce

140 g jar cream cheese
spread

1. Gently cook spinach, onion and butter in a small pan for 10 minutes.

2. Pour into a bowl and leave to cool.

3. Put mince into pan and cook, stirring, for 3 minutes.

4. Mix into spinach with corn, capsicum, breadcrumbs and egg.

5. Turn oven to 180°c (350°F). Spoon mixture into shells.

6. Spread ¼ cup spaghetti sauce in a shallow casserole dish.

7. Arrange shells in dish. Pour remaining sauce over and dot with cheese.

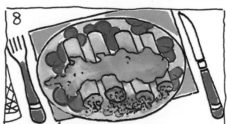

8. Bake for 40 minutes. Take out, leave 5 minutes, then serve.

Pasta is made from durum flour, a special type of "hard" flour, mixed with eggs and rolled out to make spaghetti, shells, spirals, tubes, tiny stars, cartwheels and many other shapes.

MACARONI BAKE

Serves 4

1½ cups small macaroni

1 big pan of boiling water

4 rashers of bacon

1 onion, peeled and chopped

1 x 440 g can tomato soup

½ cup milk

1 cup grated cheese

1 Gently drop macaroni into the pot of boiling water.

2 Keep it boiling well for 8 minutes.

3 Drain well. Put it into an 8-cup casserole.

4 Chop bacon. Fry gently with onion till cooked.

5 Drain it. Stir it into the casserole.

6 Stir in soup, milk and the grated cheese.

7 Bake it at 190°C (375°F) for 45 minutes.

8 Serve HOT with a tossed salad and French bread. Serves 4-5.

FABULOUS FETTUCCINE

Serves 4

375 g fettuccine
4 rashers bacon
220 g can mushrooms
   in butter sauce
130 g can creamed corn
2 medium zucchini
½ cup cream
3 spring onions, chopped
⅓ cup grated Parmesan
   cheese

1 Boil a big pot of water. Carefully add fettuccine.

2 Boil for 10 minutes. Drain well.

3 Chop bacon; throw away rinds. Fry gently.

4 Stir in mushrooms and corn.

5 Slice zucchini into rounds.

6 Add to pan with cream. Simmer for 5 minutes.

7 Add spring onions and Parmesan cheese. Stir.

Parmesan cheese is especially delicious if you grate it yourself rather than buying the already-grated stuff. It only takes a minute and you can buy whole pieces of Parmesan from the supermarket.

8 Add pasta to pan and mix well. Serve immediately.

SALMON PASTA POTS

Serves 4

1 cup small spiral pasta
210 g can pink salmon
1 small carrot
1 spring onion, finely
  chopped
¼ cup mayonnaise

⅓ cup cream
½ red capsicum,
  finely chopped
2 tablespoons chopped
  parsley

Tinned salmon is very high in calcium, especially if you eat the bones (they are quite soft and safe to eat). Calcium gives us strong bones and teeth.

1 Boil a big pot of water. Carefully add spiral pasta.

2 Boil for 10 minutes. Drain well.

3 Turn oven to 180°c (350°F).

4 Tip salmon into a mixing bowl. Mash with a fork.

5 Grate carrot over salmon. Add spring onion.

6 Add pasta, mayonnaise, cream, capsicum and parsley to bowl.

7 Spoon mixture into 4 small ovenproof pots.

Bake for 15 minutes or until heated through. Serve hot.

SPAGHETTI BOLOGNESE

Serves 4

2 tablespoons olive oil
1 medium onion, finely
  chopped
500 g minced beef
500 ml bottled spaghetti
  sauce
2 tablespoons tomato
  paste
¼ cup red wine
2 beef stock cubes,
  crumbled
½ cup frozen peas, rinsed
  and drained
2 cloves garlic, crushed
1 tablespoon finely
  chopped parsley
500 g packet spaghetti

1

Heat oil in a big heavy pan.

2

Fry onions and mince. Stir until all red has gone.

3

Add sauce, tomato paste, wine and stock cubes. Bring to boil.

4

Add peas. Turn down heat and simmer for 10 minutes.

5

Stir in garlic and parsley

6

Boil a big pot of water. Carefully add spaghetti.

7

Boil spaghetti for 10 minutes. Drain well.

Always cook spaghetti in a large pot of boiling water. The water is boiling when bubbles rise up to the surface and steam rises out of the pot.

8

Put spaghetti in a big serving bowl. Pour sauce over and serve.

SUNKEN SUBMARINES

Makes 4

2 long crusty bread rolls
2 tablespoons garlic butter
225 g can spaghetti in
    tomato and cheese
    sauce
2 thick slices devon or ham
2 slices processed cheese

1. Heat oven to 180°c (350°F). Lightly grease an oven tray.

2. Cut rolls in half and spread with butter.

3. Put rolls on tray.

4. Spoon spaghetti onto each roll.

5. Chop devon and sprinkle over spaghetti.

6. Cut cheese into thin strips.

7. Arrange cheese strips on the devon.

8. Bake for 12 minutes. Serve hot.

TUNA AND MACARONI BAKE

Serves 4

250 g macaroni
130 g corn kernels, drained
1 cup frozen peas, rinsed
  and drained
180 g can tuna in brine,
  drained

1 cup milk
22 g packet white
  sauce mix
½ cup sour cream
½ cup crushed cheese-
  flavoured biscuits

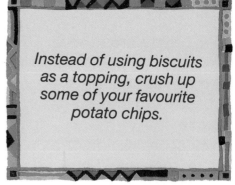

Instead of using biscuits as a topping, crush up some of your favourite potato chips.

1. Turn oven to 180°C (350°F).

2. Boil a big pot of water. Carefully add macaroni.

3. Boil macaroni for 10 minutes. Drain well.

 4. Put macaroni, corn, peas and tuna in a big bowl.

 5. Put milk and sauce mix in a small pan. Stir until it boils and thickens.

 6. Pour sauce into the bowl. Add cream. Mix well.

 7. Put in a shallow casserole. Sprinkle with biscuits.

 8. Bake for 20 minutes, then serve.

CHICKEN NOODLE OMELETTE

Serves 2

2 cups water
85 g packet chicken-
    flavoured instant noodles
1 cup chopped, cooked
    chicken

2 teaspoons finely chopped
    parsley
2 eggs, lightly beaten
2 tablespoons grated
    Cheddar cheese

Omelettes are easy to make and good for you. You can add your favourite things; try chopped tomato and ham or salami. Bean sprouts and chopped celery give lots of crunch.

1. Boil the water in a small pan.

2. Add the noodles and flavour sachet to pan.

3. Cook noodles as directed. Drain well.

4. Put noodles, chicken, parsley and eggs in a bowl. Mix well.

5. Put the mixture in a 20cm non-stick fry pan.

6. Cook for 5 minutes without stirring.

7. Sprinkle with the cheese.

8. Put under a hot grill. Cook for 2 minutes to brown. Serve hot.

Super hero saves the day!!

ASIAN BEEF AND VEGETABLES

Serves 6

750 g rump steak
2 spring onions, chopped
2 cloves garlic, crushed
2 tablespoons barbecue
  sauce
¼ cup oyster sauce
¼ teaspoon ground ginger
2 tablespoons oil
1 large onion, sliced
3 cups finely sliced
  vegetables (celery,
  broccoli, baby corn,
  carrot)

1 Trim any fat and throw it away. Cut beef into long, thin strips.

2 Put beef in a bowl. Add spring onions, garlic, barbecue and oyster sauces and ginger. Mix.

3 Heat oil in wok. Divide meat into 3 lots.

4 Add one lot of meat, stir quickly for 30 seconds.

5 Lift meat onto a plate. Repeat until all meat is cooked.

6 Add onion to wok. Stir for 2 minutes.

7 Add chopped vegetables. Stir for 3 minutes.

Stir-frying food seals in the goodness. To stir-fry, quickly move vegies or meat around the wok with a large spoon or spatula. Don't let them sit in the bottom as they will burn.

8 Add meat to wok. Stir for 5 minutes. Serve immediately with rice.

BEEF CASSEROLE

Serves 4

750 g lean stewing beef
½ cup plain flour
1 onion
1 carrot
1 beef stock cube
2 cups hot water
1 tablespoon tomato sauce

1 tablespoon
   Worcestershire sauce
1 tablespoon brown sugar
1 tablespoon vinegar
½ teaspoon ground
   nutmeg
sprinkle of salt and pepper

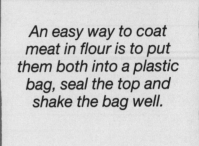

An easy way to coat meat in flour is to put them both into a plastic bag, seal the top and shake the bag well.

1 Turn oven to 180°C (350°F) Trim fat from the beef.

2 Slice the beef into bite·size cubes.

3 Toss beef in flour until each piece is coated.

4 Put in casserole. Peel + chop onion + carrot and add.

5 Dissolve stock cube in hot water. Stir in the sauces.

6 Stir in brown sugar, vinegar, nutmeg, salt and pepper.

7 Pour it all into casserole. Put the lid on.

8 Bake for 2 hours.

Serves 6

1 tablespoon oil
500 g minced beef
410 g can tomatoes,
    crushed
425 g can red kidney beans
¼ teaspoon cumin
500 g potatoes, thinly sliced
1 cup grated Cheddar
    cheese
50 g packet corn chips

1

Heat oil in a big, heavy pan. Fry mince 5 minutes.

2

Add tomatoes, kidney beans and cumin. Stir.

3

Turn down heat and simmer 15 minutes, stirring every now and then.

4

Turn oven to 180°c (350°F). In a bowl mix potatoes with cheese.

5

Layer ⅓ of the potatoes on base of an ovenproof dish. Spoon ½ the mince on top.

6

Top with another potato layer, another mince layer and finish with potatoes

7

Bake for 45 minutes.

8

Spread corn chips over top. Bake for 15 minutes more. Serve hot.

"Tex-Mex" means a dish with the typical flavours of Texas and Mexico, usually beans, beef, corn, cheese, cumin (a herb) and sometimes chilli.

CHICKEN WINGS

Serves 4

2 tablespoons lemon juice
⅓ cup soy sauce
¼ teaspoon finely grated
  fresh ginger
10 chicken wings
2 tablespoons honey
2 tablespoons tomato
  sauce

1

Mix lemon juice, soy sauce + ginger in a large flat dish.

2

Add chicken wings, turning each till coated in sauce.

3

Cover dish and leave in fridge about 5 hours.

4

Drain the wings - save the sauce.

5

In a cup mix honey, tomato sauce + rest of soy sauce mix.

6

Grill the wings for 5 minutes. Brush them thickly with the honey mixture.

7

Grill 5 minutes more. Turn wings over brush with more honey mixture.

8

Grill for 10 minutes more. Serve hot or cold.

SPARERIBS IN PLUM SAUCE

Serves 6

1 kg rack American-style
   pork spareribs
⅓ cup plum jam
1 tablespoon dark
   soy sauce
1 tablespoon Thai sweet
   chilli sauce
¼ teaspoon Chinese
   five-spice powder
3 teaspoons cornflour
½ cup chicken stock

1

Turn oven to 200°C (400°F).

2

Put ribs onto a rack in a shallow baking dish.

3
Bake for 25 minutes. Turn ribs once during cooking.

4
Heat jam, soy and chilli sauce and five-spice powder in a small pan.

5

Mix cornflour and chicken stock together until smooth.

6

Pour into pan. Stir gently until plum sauce boils and thickens.

7

When ribs are cooked, pull ribs apart. Arrange on a serving dish.

American-style spareribs are thinner and less fatty than pork spareribs. If you use pork spareribs for this recipe, trim most of the fat away before you cook them.

8

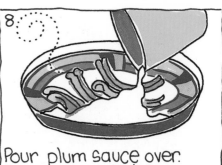
Pour plum sauce over. Serve immediately.

SAVOURY RICE

Serves 6

1 tablespoon oil
1 onion, chopped
1 x 425 g can peeled
   tomato pieces (and the
   juice)
1 teaspoon instant chicken
   stock powder

sprinkle of salt and pepper
¼ teaspoon sugar
1 x 310 g can whole kernel
   corn
3½ cups cooked rice
1 cup frozen peas
1 cup grated Cheddar
   cheese

If the tomato pieces are big, put them into a bowl and use a potato masher to break them up.

1. Turn oven to 180°C.(350°F) Grease an ovenproof dish.

2. Heat oil in a pan. Add onion. Fry gently.

3. Add tomatoes, stock, salt pepper and sugar.

4. Stir it over low heat for 7 minutes.

5. Drain corn. Mix in a bowl with rice + peas.

6. Spread rice, corn and peas in the dish.

7. Pour tomato mixture over rice.

8. Sprinkle cheese over. Bake for 30 minutes.

LAMB AND APRICOT PARCELS

Makes 6
100 g dried apricots, finely chopped
500 g minced lamb
½ cup apricot conserve
½ cup herb stuffing mix
3 sheets ready-rolled puff pastry
1 egg, lightly beaten

1

Turn oven to 180°c (350°F).

2

Mix apricots, lamb, conserve and stuffing mix. Leave 20 minutes.

3

Shape mince into 6 flat, square patties, about 10cm × 10cm.

4

Cut pastry sheets in ½ to make 6 pieces. Put a pattie on the end of each piece.

5

Brush pastry with beaten egg.

6

Fold over pattie. Press edges together. Trim edges.

7

Cut 3 slits in top of each parcel with a sharp knife.

8

Brush with egg. Bake for 30 minutes until crisp and golden.

SALMON MORNAY

Serves 4

1½ cups cooked rice
1 x 210 g can pink salmon
1 hard-boiled egg
50 g butter
2 tablespoons plain flour
1½ cups milk
⅓ cup grated cheddar
    cheese
sprinkle of salt and pepper
¼ cup dry breadcrumbs

1

Turn oven to 180°C (350°F)
Spread rice in baking dish.

2

Drain salmon. Remove bones.
Chop up. Spread on rice.

3

Chop egg. Sprinkle over the
salmon. Melt butter in a
small pan.

4

Stir in flour until smooth.
Take off heat. Stir in milk.

5

Reheat, stirring all the time
until it boils.

6

Stir in cheese, salt and pepper.
Pour it over the salmon and rice.

7

Sprinkle crumbs evenly
over. Bake for 20 minutes.

*Tuna may be used
instead of pink salmon
for this recipe.*

8

Serve it
hot
with a
tossed salad

Serves 4

SAUSAGE AND BEAN BAKE

Serves 4
1 large onion
3 slices bacon,
2 sticks celery, sliced
4 continental sausages,
  sliced
2 spring onions, finely
  chopped

1 tablespoon finely
  chopped parsley
225 g can baked beans in
  tomato sauce
1 tablespoon tomato paste
½ cup water

Serve this dish with a crispy green salad and hot bread rolls. Put rolls on an oven tray; place in the oven for the last 15 minutes of cooking time.

1 Turn oven to 180°c (350°F).

2 Chop onion and bacon finely. (Throw away bacon rind.)

3 Mix onion, bacon, celery and sausage in a big bowl.

4 Add spring onions and parsley. Mix well.

5 Stir in baked beans, tomato paste and water.

6 Spread mixture into a shallow ovenproof dish.

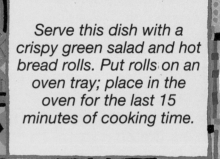

7 Put lid on or cover with foil. Bake 20 minutes.

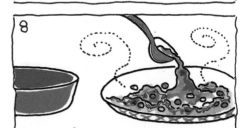

8 Take off lid or foil and bake for 15 minutes more. Serve hot.

Makes 12

6 chicken thighs, skinned, boned
2 teaspoons soy sauce
⅓ cup crunchy peanut butter
2 tablespoons lemon juice
150 g can coconut cream
1 tablespoon sweet chilli sauce
¼ teaspoon garam masala

1. Cut chicken in long, thin strips.

2. Put chicken and soy sauce in a bowl. Stir to cover chicken with sauce.

3. In another bowl, mix peanut butter and lemon juice together.

4. Add coconut cream, chilli sauce and garam masala. Mix well.

5. Mix 2 tablespoons peanut sauce into chicken.

6. Thread chicken onto skewers.

7. Grill for 3 minutes. Turn chicken and grill other side for 3 minutes.

Buy packets of bamboo or metal skewers from the supermarket. Soak the bamboo skewers in water to prevent them burning under the hot grill. Use gloves to pick up hot skewers.

8. Put peanut sauce in a small pan. Cook 5 minutes until hot. Spoon over chicken and serve.

POTATO SALAD

Serves 6

6 medium potatoes
1 x 310 g can whole kernel
  corn
¼ cup chopped parsley
sprinkle of salt and pepper
1 tablespoon bottled
  French dressing
¼ cup mayonnaise

Scrub the potatoes until they are clean.

2

Boil them in water until tender.

3

When cool, peel them and cut into cubes.

4

Put cubes into a nice salad bowl.

5
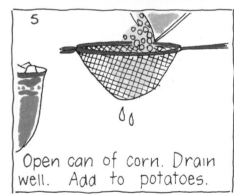

Open can of corn. Drain well. Add to potatoes.

6

Add the parsley, the salt and the pepper.

7

Stir in French dressing and the mayonnaise.

8

Gently mix it all and serve cold.

FRIED RICE

Serves 4

1/3 cup oil
1 cup long-grain rice
1 1/2 cups chicken stock
1/2 cup frozen peas, rinsed
   and drained
1/2 medium red capsicum,
   finely sliced
100 g button mushrooms,
   thinly sliced
2 eggs, lightly beaten
2 spring onions, chopped
200 g can peeled prawns
1 tablespoon soy sauce
2 teaspoons sesame oil

1
Heat 2 tablespoons oil in a pan. Add rice. Stir 5 minutes or until golden.

2
Pour in stock. Turn down heat, put lid on. Simmer 15 minutes or until rice is tender.

3
Add peas. Cover and put to one side.

4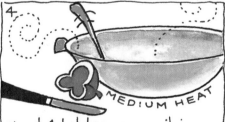
Heat 1 tablespoon oil in wok. Add capsicum. Stir 1 minute. Drain on paper towels.

5
Add rest of oil. Add mushrooms. Stir 1 minute. Drain with capsicum.

6
Add eggs. Swirl over base — don't stir.

7
When cooked like an omelette, lift out and slice.

When heating oil, smoke means the oil is too hot and will burn food. Turn down heat and gently take the pan off the heat for a few minutes before adding food.

8
Put all ingredients into wok. Add soy sauce and sesame oil. Stir until hot.

MICROWAVE MIRACLES

TUNA BURGERS

Serves 4

185 g tin of tuna, in brine
½ cup grated Cheddar cheese
¼ cup mayonnaise
1 tablespoon tomato sauce
1 tablespoon lemon juice
ground pepper
4 hamburger buns — halved
butter

1

Drain tuna well. Put it in a bowl.

2

Add cheese, mayonnaise, tomato sauce, + lemon.

3

Add pepper. Mix it all together well.

4

Butter the buns lightly.

5

Spread mixture evenly on 4 halves.

6

Put the top on each burger.

7

Wrap each one in absorbent paper.

8

Cook (2 at a time) on High for 1½ minutes.

CHEESY SAUSAGE SLICE

Serves 4

4 slices wholemeal bread,
  buttered one side
2 continental frankfurts
  or 1 stick cabanossi
1 small onion
1 small zucchini
1 tablespoon self-raising
  flour
2 teaspoons finely chopped
  parsley
2 eggs, lightly beaten
½ cup grated mozzarella
  cheese

1. Cut crusts off bread.

2. Arrange, butter side up, on bottom of a shallow, round 23cm dish.

3. Cut frankfurts or cabanossi into thin slices.

4. Coarsely grate onion and zucchini into a bowl.

5. Add frankfurts or cabanossi, flour and parsley. Mix well.

6. Add eggs and cheese. Stir well.

7. Spoon over bread. Cover with plastic wrap.

8. Cook on a rack on Medium High for 8 minutes. Serve hot or cold.

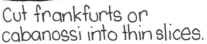

To save time, grate cheese beforehand. Hold grater over a plate and grate the amount needed. Cover with plastic wrap, store in refrigerator.

HAM AND CHEESE BREAD

Serves 6

1 French stick (about 25 cm long)

8–10 slices cheese, thinly sliced

8–10 slices ham

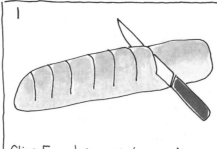

1

Slice French bread (not quite through) 8 or 10 times.

2

Trim cheese to about the size of diameter of bread.

3

Trim ham to about the same size.

4

Place ham + cheese together in each cut.

5

Put on a paper towel.

6

Cook on High 1–2 minutes.

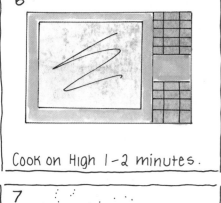

7

Watch for cheese to start melting, then take out.

8

Serve cut through.

CHEESE SAUCE

Makes 2 cups

50 g butter
¼ cup plain flour
2 cups milk
½ cup grated Cheddar
  cheese
ground pepper

1 Put butter in a bowl. Cover with absorbent paper.

2 Cook on Medium (50% power) for 2 minutes till melted

3 Add the flour. Stir in well.

4 Add the milk. Whisk it in well.

5 Cook (uncovered) on High for 2 minutes. Whisk well.

6 Cook on High for 3½ minutes, whisking once.

7 Stir in cheese + pepper Stir well.

8 Serve spooned over hot vegetables.

PITTA SNACK

Serves 1
1 small pitta bread
2 teaspoons tomato paste
 (or chutney)

1 slice Swiss cheese
2 slices ham
1 teaspoon chopped spring
 onion

1
Put pitta bread on plate.

2
Spread with tomato
paste or chutney.

3
Slice cheese thinly

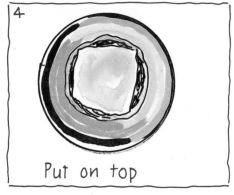

4
Put on top

5
Chop ham finely

6
Sprinkle over

7
Sprinkle chopped spring
onion over.

8
Cook on High 30 seconds
until cheese melts.

CHEESE AND POTATO BAKE

Serves 6

30 g butter
1 onion, peeled and
  chopped
6 medium-sized potatoes
sprinkle of salt and pepper
⅔ cup milk
¾ cup grated Cheddar
  cheese

1
Put butter + onion in a bowl.
Cook on High 3 minutes.

2
Peel the potatoes. Slice them
up thinly.

3
Put half the potatoes into a 22cm
round casserole.

4
Spread onion + butter over.
Sprinkle with salt + pepper.

5
Arrange rest of potatoes evenly
over.

6
Pour the milk over.
Sprinkle cheese on top.

7
Cover with cling wrap. Prick.
Cook on High for 8 minutes.

8
Remove cover.

Cook on High for 10 minutes
or until tender.

If you like, put under
grill to brown cheese
and serve.

MARBLE CAKE

Makes 1 x 20 cm cake

340 g packet vanilla cake mix
1/3 cup plain flour, sifted
1 tablespoon cocoa powder, sifted
2-3 drops strawberry essence
2-3 drops red food colouring

ICING
1 1/4 cups icing sugar
30 g butter, melted
1 tablespoon milk

1 Grease a 20cm microwave ring mould or a round microwave dish.

2 Make up cake mix following the microwave directions on the packet. Fold in flour and divide mixture into 3 bowls.

3 Add the cocoa powder to one bowl and mix well.

4 Add the strawberry essence and red food colouring to the second bowl. Leave the mixture in the third bowl plain.

5 Put a tablespoon of each mixture alternately into the cake ring until all the mixture is used up.

6 Use a skewer to lightly swirl the colours together so it looks like marble – THIS IS HOW THE CAKE GETS ITS NAME

7 Microwave on High 4-5 minutes, until the cake feels spongy. Ice cake.

You can make marble cakes in any colour, depending on which food colouring you use. How about a green and blue cake to amaze your parents or friends?

8 TO MAKE COLOURED ICING:
beat together the icing ingredients then divide into bowls and add red food colouring or cocoa powder.

CUSTARD

Serves 4

3 tablespoons caster sugar
2 tablespoons custard
  powder
1½ cups milk
2 egg yolks
1 teaspoon imitation vanilla
  essence

1 Put sugar + custard powder in a 4 cup size bowl.

2 Add the milk and whisk it all well.

3 Cook on Medium (50%) for 3 minutes. Whisk well.

4 Cook on Medium (50%) for 4 minutes. Whisk well.

5 Add the egg yolks. Whisk well.

6 Cook on Medium (50%) for 1½ minutes, stirring twice.

7 Stir in the vanilla.

8 Serve hot or cold with fruits or puddings.

CHOCOLATE FUDGE SAUCE

Makes 2 cups

125 g dark chocolate, finely
   chopped
400 g can sweetened
   condensed milk
100 g white marshmallows

1
Put chocolate and condensed milk in a medium bowl.

2
Cook on Medium (50%) for 1 minute. Stir.

3
Cut marshmallows into small pieces.

4
Stir into chocolate mixture.

5
Cook on Medium (50%) for 1 minute.

6
Beat until almost smooth.

7
Cook on Medium (50%) for 1 minute. Stir.

8
Serve hot or cold with ice-cream.

PAVLOVA

Serves 6-8

4 egg whites (at room
   temperature)
1 cup caster sugar
½ teaspoon imitation vanilla
   essence
½ teaspoon vinegar
whipped cream + fruit

1.
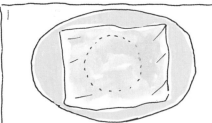
Take turntable out of oven.
Put a sheet of baking paper
on it. Mark an 18cm circle.

2.

Beat the egg whites
until soft peaks form.

3.

Sprinkle in half the
sugar. Beat well.

4.

Slowly add rest of sugar.
Beat until dissolved.

5.

Add vanilla + vinegar.
Beat in well.

6.

Spoon mixture onto paper.
Form into a circle.
Put back in the oven.

7.

Cook it on HIGH 2 minutes.
Open oven door + leave it
there for 10 minutes.

8.

Carefully take it out
of oven + leave until
cold.
Carefully peel
off the paper + put on
a plate.
Put whipped cream + fruit on.

CHOCOLATE PUDDING

Serves 4

2 tablespoons butter
2 tablespoons caster sugar
1 egg, lightly beaten
1/2 teaspoon vanilla essence
2/3 cup self-raising flour
1/4 cup milk
2 tablespoons cocoa powder

1 tablespoon hot water

SAUCE
1/4 cup water
2 tablespoons sugar
3 tablespoons butter
3/4 cup dark choc bits

1
Put butter, sugar, egg, vanilla, flour and milk in a bowl. Mix until it's smooth.

2
Mix together the cocoa and water to make a paste. Add it to the mixture and stir well.

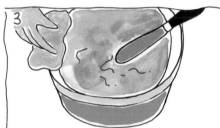

3
Smooth the surface of the mixture and wipe the top of the bowl clean.

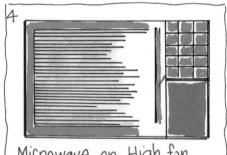

4
Microwave on High for 5 minutes.

5
SAUCE: Mix together the water, sugar, butter and Choc bits in a large jug.

6
Microwave on High 1 minute. Stir until it's smooth then cook 1 more minute until it's thick.

7
Pour sauce over pudding. DON'T STIR IT! Leave it for 1 minute then microwave on medium (50%) for 1 minute.

8
Sprinkle pudding with icing sugar and serve it warm with cream or ice cream.

GINGER SLICE

Makes about 12 slices

125 g butter
¼ cup caster sugar
1 cup plain flour
½ teaspoon baking powder
½ teaspoon ground ginger

TOPPING
15 g butter
1 tablespoon golden syrup
½ teaspoon imitation vanilla
essence
1 teaspoon ground ginger
⅓ cup icing sugar

Fruit cooked by microwave is sweeter and has better flavour than stewed fruit. Try cooking a single piece of fruit in its own skin, a peach maybe, but not for too long.

1. Beat butter and sugar until smooth.

2. Sift in flour, baking powder + ginger. Mix it all well.

3. Mix to a dough. Knead until a smooth dough has formed.

4. Press firmly into 20cm casserole. Cook on Medium High (75% power) 6 minutes.

5. **TOPPING:** Put butter + golden syrup in a bowl. Cook on High 30 seconds.

6. Stir in vanilla, ginger and icing sugar. Whisk well.

7. Spread it evenly over the hot base.

8. Leave it until cold and then slice.

SPIKY CRACKLES

Makes 16 squares

250 g packet jersey
   caramels, chopped
1 tablespoon golden syrup
60 g butter
250 g dark chocolate, finely
   chopped
3 cups Rice Bubbles
100 g white marshmallows,
   chopped
⅓ cup toasted slivered
   almonds

1

Line base and sides of a 23cm square dish with foil. (Don't put this in the microwave!)

2

Put caramels, golden syrup, butter and ½ the chocolate in a bowl.

3

Cook (uncovered) on Medium for 2 minutes. Stir until smooth.

4

Mix Rice Bubbles into caramel. Press into dish.

5

Put remaining chocolate and marshmallows in a bowl.

6

Cook on Medium 45 seconds. Beat until smooth.

7

Spread over caramel mixture. Press nuts on top.

Chocolate comes originally from Central America and Mexico, where the ancient Aztecs made it into a thick drink flavoured with vanilla.

8
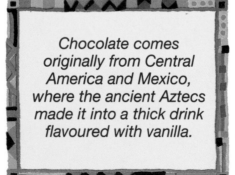
Leave to set, cut into fingers and serve.

MUESLI BARS

Makes 12 pieces

1 cup desiccated coconut
1 cup unsalted peanuts
1 cup sunflower seeds
1 cup sesame seeds
1 cup rolled oats
125 g butter
½ cup brown sugar
¼ cup honey

1. Put coconut, peanuts, seeds, oats in big, flat bowl.

2. Cook on High 5 minutes.

3. Put butter, sugar, honey in another bowl.

4. Cover with absorbent paper. Cook 4½ minutes on Medium (50%).

5. Stir well. Add to mix in big bowl. Stir well.

6. Spread evenly in a 20cm × 30cm lined tin.

7. Press down firmly. (Try using the bottom of a cup.)

8. Leave till cold, then slice into bars.

CHOCOLATE FUDGE

Makes 36 pieces
125 g butter, melted
2 cups sugar
²/₃ cup evaporated milk
2 cups tiny marshmallows
1 cup choc bits
½ teaspoon vanilla essence
½ cup coconut

1 Line a 20cm square tin with foil.

2 Put melted butter in a large bowl. Stir in sugar + evaporated milk.

3 Microwave on High for 7-10 minutes. Stir every 3 minutes + scrape the side of bowl. BE CAREFUL IT'S VERY HOT!

4 Add marshmallows, chocolate and vanilla essence.

5 Stir until the chocolate and the marshmallows have melted. Add coconut.

6 Pour the mixture into the tin. Mark it into squares while it's still warm.

7 Leave it to cool, then cover it and put it in the refrigerater for a few hours.

8 Cut the fudge into squares when it is set.

COCOA MALLOW

Serves 1

½ teaspoon cocoa powder
1 teaspoon sugar
3 tablespoons hot water
about 1 cup of milk
1 white marshmallow

1 Put cocoa in a mug

2 Add sugar + hot water

3 Stir well.

4 Cook on High 30 seconds

5 Stir well.

6 Add milk to fill mug ¾ full.

7 Cook on High 90 seconds

8 Pop marshmallow on top.

CAPPUCCINO

Serves 4

2 cups milk
4 teaspoons grated
  chocolate
4 teaspoons sugar
2 teaspoons instant coffee
⅓ cup cream, whipped
drinking chocolate powder

1

Put milk in a 4-cup glass jug.

2

Microwave on High 3-3½ minutes till hot but not boiling.

3

Add grated chocolate + sugar. Stir it well.

4

Stir in instant coffee. Stir very well.

5

Pour into 4 mugs.

6

Top with cream.

7

Sprinkle with drinking chocolate powder.

8

Serve with cookies.

HOT CHOCOLATE

Serves 3

3 cups milk
⅓ cup grated dark
   chocolate
1 tablespoon sugar
1 egg
drinking chocolate powder

1 Put milk in big jug. Microwave on High 2 minutes.

2 Add chocolate + sugar. Whisk.

3 Whisk egg in a cup

4 Add to jug. Whisk.

5 Microwave on High – about 3–4 minutes till foamy – don't boil it!

6 Whisk well.

7 Pour into 3 mugs.

8 Sprinkle with a little drinking chocolate powder.

CAKES AND BISCUITS

FUDGE CAKE

Makes 1 x 20 cm cake
1½ cups self-raising flour
3 tablespoons cocoa powder
1 cup caster sugar
1 cup water
1 teaspoon imitation vanilla
 essence
1 tablespoon white vinegar
½ cup vegetable oil

1

Turn oven to 180°C (350°F)
Grease a 20cm fluted
ring tin.

2

Dust the inside of the
tin with a little flour.

3

Put 1¾ cups flour, cocoa,
sugar + water in a bowl.

4

Add vanilla, vinegar and oil.

5

Mix it all together with
a whisk.

6

When smooth, pour it
into the tin.

7

Bake 35-40 minutes. Cool for
10 minutes then take out of tin.

8   ICING
Mix: 1 cup icing sugar
 1½ tablespoons cocoa
 1 tablespoon butter
with a little hot water.
(Use more water if you
want the icing runny.)
Ice the cake.

DOUBLE CHOCOLATE CAKE

Makes one 23 cm cake

125 g butter, softened
¾ cup caster sugar
2 eggs
1¼ cups self-raising flour
2 tablespoons custard powder
⅓ cup cocoa powder
½ cup water
BUTTERCREAM
125 g butter
1⅓ cups icing sugar, sifted
½ cup cocoa powder
2 tablespoons milk

1

Turn oven to 180°C (350°F). Grease a deep 23 cm round cake tin.

2

Put butter, sugar, eggs, flour, custard powder and cocoa in mixing bowl.

3

Add water. Beat 2 minutes on low speed, then 4 minutes on high speed.

4

Spread evenly in tin. Bake 40 minutes. Turn onto a rack to cool.

5

Put butter, icing sugar, cocoa and milk in a small bowl.

6

Beat 1 minute on low speed, then 4 minutes on high speed.

7

Cut cake in half. Spread buttercream on bottom half.

Decorate this cake with chocolate buttons, chocolate animals or whatever takes your fancy.

8

Cover with cake top. Spread buttercream over top and sides.

TROPICAL CARROT LOAF

Makes one 25 cm loaf

1½ cups grated carrot
225 g can pineapple
    pieces, drained
1 teaspoon grated
    orange rind
2 cups wholemeal
    self-raising flour
¾ cup oil

3 eggs, lightly beaten
⅔ cup caster sugar
1 teaspoon cinnamon
½ teaspoon mixed spice
TOPPING
250 g cream cheese
1 teaspoon grated
    orange rind
½ cup icing sugar

To decorate cake, draw a carrot shape in the icing with a skewer. Carefully fill in the outline with coloured sprinkles.

1 Turn oven to 180°C (350°F). Grease a 25×15cm loaf tin. Line with waxed paper.

2 Put carrot, pineapple, rind, flour, oil, eggs, sugar and spices in a big bowl.

3 Mix well with a fork.

4 Spread evenly in tin. Bake for 55 minutes.

5 Turn cake out and cool on a wire rack.

6 Put cream cheese, rind and icing sugar in a small bowl.

7 Beat until light and fluffy.

8 Turn cake right-side up. Spread topping over cake.

STICKY BUNS

Makes 12

60 g butter
½ cup brown sugar } Step 1
2 tablespoons sultanas
2¼ cups plain flour
2 teaspoons baking powder
30 g butter (Step 3)

2 ripe bananas, mashed
½ cup milk
30 g butter, melted
2 tablespoons
  brown sugar } Step 6

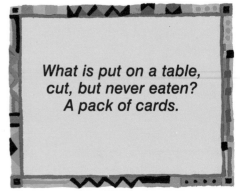

What is put on a table, cut, but never eaten? A pack of cards.

1
Turn oven to 190°C(375°F). Melt the 60g butter + the ½ cup brown sugar in a pan.

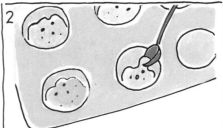

2
Stir in sultanas. Spoon mixture into base of 12 deep muffin pans.

3
Sift flour + baking powder into bowl. Rub in the 30g butter till it looks crumbly.

4
Add mashed bananas + milk. Mix it all quickly to form a soft dough.

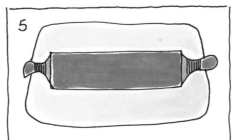

5
Knead it. Roll out on floured surface till it's 20 x 15 cm.

6
Spread melted butter over. Sprinkle brown sugar over.

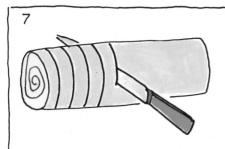

7
Firmly roll up (from long side). Cut neatly into 12 slices.

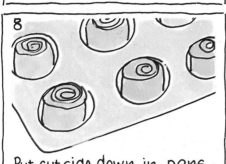

8
Put cut-side down in pans. Bake 12-15 minutes.

LEMON BUTTERFLY CAKES

Makes about 35

340 g packet buttercake
  mix
2 teaspoons grated
  lemon rind
⅔ cup bottled lemon butter
½ cup thickened cream
¼ cup icing sugar
35 silver balls

1 Turn oven to 180°c (350°F). Lay out 35 paper patty cases.

2 Follow directions on packet to make cake batter. Mix in the rind.

3 Put 1 tablespoon batter into each patty case. Bake for 15 minutes. Cool on wire rack.

4 Cut a circle from the top of each cake. Cut circles in half.

5 Put ½ teaspoon lemon butter into each cake.

6 Put cream in a small bowl. Beat until firm peaks form.

7 Put 1 tablespoon cream onto each cake. Press the half-circles on top.

8 Dust with icing sugar. Put a silver ball on top.

78

PATTY CAKES

Makes about 30

2 cups self-raising flour
¾ cup sugar
125 g soft butter
3 eggs
½ cup milk
½ teaspoon vanilla
essence

1
Turn oven to 180°C (350°F)
Set out 30 paper patty cases

2
Sift flour, sugar into
mixing bowl.

3
Add butter, eggs, milk
and vanilla.

4
Beat it all very fast
until it's quite smooth.

5
Fill patty cases until
¾ full with the mixture.

6
Bake for 15 minutes
until golden.

7
Cool on a wire rack
and then ice them.

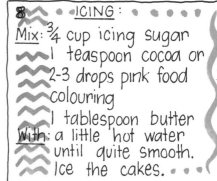
8 • • • ICING: • • • • • •
Mix: ¾ cup icing sugar
1 teaspoon cocoa or
2-3 drops pink food
colouring
1 tablespoon butter
With: a little hot water
until quite smooth.
Ice the cakes. • • • •

LEMON SLICE

Makes about 14 slices

100 g butter
¼ cup icing sugar
1 cup plain flour

TOPPING
2 eggs
2 tablespoons lemon juice
2 teaspoons grated lemon rind
1 cup caster sugar
2 tablespoons plain flour
½ teaspoon baking powder
1 tablespoon icing sugar

1
Turn oven to 180°C (350°F)
Grease a 30 × 20cm tin.

2
Beat butter and icing sugar until smooth.

3
Sift in the 1 cup flour. Mix well to a smooth dough.

4
Press it evenly in the tin. Bake it for 20 minutes. Set aside to cool.

5
TOPPING:
Beat the eggs well. Stir in lemon juice + lemon rind.

6
Sift in the caster sugar, the 2 tablespoons of flour + baking powder. Stir till mixed.

7
Pour it over the base. Bake again for 25 minutes.

8
Cool it.
✿
Sift icing sugar on top and cut into squares

Lemon Slice can be served with whipped cream or ice-cream for dessert.

CHUNKY CHOCOLATE COOKIES

Makes 16

½ cup brown sugar
1 egg
⅓ cup oil
2 tablespoons cocoa powder
½ cup self-raising flour
½ cup plain flour
⅓ cup choc bits
60 g white chocolate,
   chopped

1. Turn oven to 180°c (350°F). Lightly grease 2 biscuit trays.

2. Put sugar, egg and oil in a mixing bowl. Mix well with a fork.

3. Sift cocoa and flours into bowl.

4. Add chocolates. Mix through gently.

5. Knead lightly with hands to make a soft dough.

6. Make balls by rolling 1 tablespoon of dough.

7. Put balls on tray 4cm apart. Bake 1 tray at a time for 12 minutes.

8. Leave on tray 5 minutes, then cool on wire rack.

ANZAC BISCUITS

Makes about 25

2 cups rolled oats
2 cups plain flour
2 cups desiccated coconut
1½ cups caster sugar
250 g butter
4 tablespoons golden syrup
1 teaspoon baking soda
2 tablespoons boiling water

1. Turn oven to 160°C(325°F). Lightly grease oven trays.

2. Put oats, flour, coconut, sugar in big mixing bowl.

3. Melt butter + golden syrup in pan, stirring. Take off heat.

4. Mix baking soda + boiling water in a cup.

5. Add to melted butter in the pan.

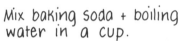

6. Quickly add to big bowl. Mix it all well.

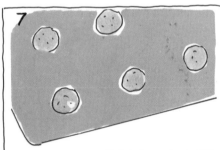

7. Roll tablespoonful lots into balls. Put on trays 5 cm apart.

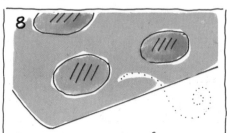

8. Press lightly with fork. Bake 20 minutes– one tray at a time.

VANILLA SLICE

Makes 9

250 g Morning Coffee biscuits
2 cups milk
1 cup cream
85 g packet instant vanilla
   pudding mix
1½ cups icing sugar, sifted
2 tablespoons passionfruit
   pulp
60 g butter, melted

1 Line a deep 19cm square cake tin with foil.

2 Arrange a row of biscuits over the bottom.

3 Put milk and cream in a small mixing bowl. Sprinkle pudding mix on top.

4 Beat 5 minutes on medium speed. Pour over biscuits.

5 Top with another layer of biscuits (wrong side up).

6 Beat icing sugar, passionfruit and butter in a small bowl until smooth.

7 Spread over biscuits.

8 Put in fridge overnight before cutting. Cut into 9 slices to serve.

LEMON COOKIES

Makes about 48

¼ cup milk
1 teaspoon vinegar
125 g butter
¾ cup sugar
1 egg

1 teaspoon grated lemon rind
1¾ cups plain flour
1 teaspoon baking powder
¼ teaspoon salt

To decorate these cookies, cut thin strips of orange or lemon peel and arrange on top before the icing sets.

1
Turn oven to 180°C (350°F). Mix milk + vinegar in cup. Set aside to turn sour.

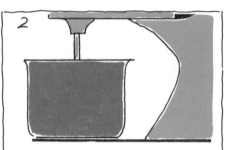
2
Beat butter, sugar, egg + lemon rind until smooth.

3
Sift in flour, baking powder and salt.

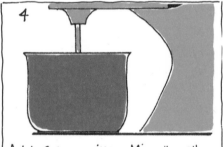
4
Add sour milk. Mix it all together well.

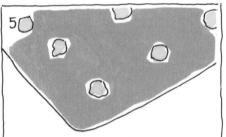
5
Put teaspoonful lots 5cm apart on an oven tray.

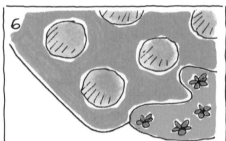
6
Bake 12 minutes or until golden (Bake 1 tray at a time)

7
Lift off tray. Cool on a wire rack. Makes about 48.

8 ●●● Glaze ●●●●
Mix ½ cup icing sugar + 2 tablespoons lemon juice until mixed + smooth

Spread on hot cookie + ● leave until cold. ●

BIRTHDAY CAKE

Makes 1 x 20 cm cake

125 g butter
¾ cup caster sugar
2 eggs, lightly beaten
1 teaspoon vanilla essence
2 cups self-raising flour
½ cup milk

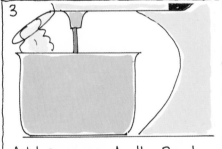

1

Turn oven to 180°C. Grease a 20cm round or heart-shaped tin. Line base with waxed paper.

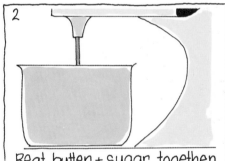

2

Beat butter + sugar together until smooth + creamy.

3

Add eggs gradually. Beat well each time you add.

4

Add the vanilla essence. Beat it all well.

5

Gently fold in alternate spoonfuls of flour and milk until it's all added.

6

Stir until it's smooth. Spread evenly in tin. Bake 40 minutes.

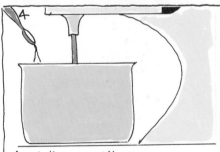

7

Stick a skewer into the middle of the cake to check it's cooked – the skewer should come out clean.

8

Cool in tin 10 minutes, then turn out + cool completely on wire rack.

Mix 1½ cups icing sugar, 1 tablespoon butter + enough hot water to mix till smooth.
Spread over cake.
Decorate with jelly beans.

The Great Entertainer

DESSERTS AND SWEET TREATS

CHOCO BANANA SPLIT

Serves 4

¾ cup caster sugar
3 tablespoons cocoa powder
2 tablespoons water
¾ cup evaporated milk
2 tablespoons butter
½ teaspoon imitation vanilla essence
4 medium-sized bananas
4 scoops vanilla ice-cream

1

Put sugar, cocoa, and water in a small pan.

2

LOW HEAT
Add milk. Stir it until it comes to the boil.

3

LOW HEAT
Simmer gently for 5 minutes. Stir in butter and vanilla.

4

Set it aside to cool for about 10 minutes.

5

Peel, then split the bananas in half.

6
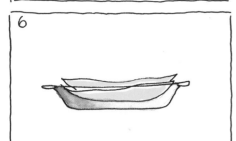
Put 2 halves in each of 4 nice sundae dishes.

7
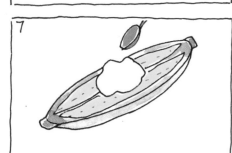
Put a scoop of ice-cream on top of each.

8

Pour chocolate sauce over each and serve.

RASPBERRY ROYALE

Serves 6

85 g strawberry instant
  pudding mix
1 cup milk
2 teaspoons gelatine
1 tablespoon boiling water
300 ml thickened cream,
  whipped
$1/2$ cup fresh raspberries
250 g packet jam sponge roll

1

Line a medium bowl with plastic wrap.

2

Beat together the pudding mix and milk in a large bowl until smooth.

3

Put the gelatine + boiling water in a small bowl + stir gently until dissolved.

4

Mix gently into the pudding mixture. Add the whipped cream.

5

Add raspberries. Mix gently.

6

Cut cake into 1 cm slices. Cover bottom and sides of serving bowl.

7

Spread raspberry filling on top of cake. Cover with plastic wrap.

Always read the recipe through before you start cooking. Note how long it will take, and work out if you have time to make the dish. Try and plan your cooking well ahead.

8

Put in fridge overnight. Turn out onto a flat plate to serve.

ROCKY ROAD ICE-CREAM

Serves 6

100 g packet red glacé cherries
100 g packet coloured marshmallows
¼ cup choc bits
¼ cup crushed nuts

2 tablespoons desiccated coconut
1 L vanilla ice-cream, softened
60 g dark chocolate, chopped

This ice-cream makes a great sundae. Fill a long glass with a scoop of rocky road, sliced bananas, more ice-cream and top with chocolate sauce.

1 Chop cherries finely.

2 Cut marshmallows into pieces.

3 Put cherries, marshmallows, choc bits, nuts and coconut in a big bowl.

4 Add ice-cream. Mix gently.

5 Pour into a loaf or bread tin. Smooth the top.

6 Cover with plastic wrap. Put in freezer for 3 hours.

7 Melt dark chocolate in a bowl over hot water.

8 Spoon melted chocolate over ice-cream and serve.

FRUIT FLUMMERY

Serves 6

½ cup cold water
1 tablespoon gelatine
¼ cup plain flour
¾ cup caster sugar
½ cup apple juice
1 teaspoon lemon juice
1 cup hot water
the pulp of 4 passionfruit
plain yoghurt, to serve

1

Whisk cold water + gelatine. Set aside.

2

Put flour + sugar in small pan. Add apple juice. Whisk.

3

Add lemon juice + hot water. Whisk.

4

Stir over heat until it's thick and bubbly.

MEDIUM HEAT

5

Take off heat. Add the gelatine. Whisk well.

6

Pour into a bowl. Chill in fridge till it thickens. DON'T let it set!

7

Beat it hard (about 5 minutes) until very thick and pale.

8

Stir in ¾ of the passionfruit pulp. Put into glasses and put in fridge to set.

Serve with yoghurt and the rest of the passionfruit pulp.

CHOC-HONEYCOMB MOUSSE

Serves 4
½ cup thickened cream
250 g milk chocolate,
  chopped
¼ cup sugar
2 teaspoons gelatine
½ cup water
2 x 35 g chocolate-
  coated honeycomb
  bars, chopped

1. Heat cream gently in a small pan.

2. Add chocolate. Take off heat and stir until chocolate melts.

3. Pour into mixing bowl. Put aside to cool.

4. Mix sugar, gelatine and water in a small pan. Stir until sugar dissolves.

5. Turn up heat and boil. Take off heat and pour into mixing bowl.

6. Beat on Medium speed 10 minutes until thick and fluffy.

7. Gently mix chocolate through. Spoon mousse into 4 dishes.

8. Put in fridge for 30 minutes. Sprinkle honeycomb over and serve.

FRUIT CRUMBLE

Serves 6

1 cup canned peach slices
1 cup pineapple pieces
50 g butter
½ cup brown sugar
1 cup bran
1 cup cornflakes
cream or ice-cream, to
   serve

1

Turn oven to 180°C (350°F).
Drain peaches + pineapples.

2

Put the fruit into an
ovenproof dish.

3

Put butter in a pan.
Melt on low heat.

4

Take off heat. Stir in
brown sugar.

5

Add bran + cornflakes.
Stir it well.

6

Sprinkle it evenly
over the fruit.

7

Bake for 12 – 15 minutes.

8

Serve warm with
cream or ice-cream.

93

BLUEBERRY PIKELETS

Makes about 14

1 cup self-raising flour
2 tablespoons caster sugar
1 teaspoon grated lemon
   rind
1 egg, lightly beaten
1/3 cup sour cream
1/2 cup milk
1 teaspoon oil
1 cup fresh blueberries
1/2 cup maple syrup

1
Sift flour into a mixing bowl. Stir in sugar and rind.

2
Add egg, cream and milk.

3
NO LUMPS!
Beat until mixture is smooth, with no lumps.

4
LOW HEAT
Brush a non-stick fry pan with oil. Heat until warm.

5
LOW HEAT
Drop a tablespoon of batter in. Shape into a circle about 8cm wide.

6
Cook 2 minutes; turn and cook other side 2 minutes until golden.

7
As the pikelets are cooked pile them up on a plate and cover with foil to keep warm.

8
Serve with blueberries piled on. Pour maple syrup over.

Make pikelet batter the day before, cover bowl with plastic wrap and place in fridge. A good idea if you are cooking them for breakfast, because you don't have to get up so early.

Makes about 12

1 cup plain flour
sprinkle of salt
1 egg
1¼ cups milk
a little oil to grease frypan
lemon juice ⎫ to sprinkle
sugar ⎬ over pancakes
cream or ice-cream, to serve

1 Sift flour + salt into mixing bowl. Add egg and milk.

2 NO LUMPS! Whisk + whisk till smooth. Set aside for 1 hour.

3 MEDIUM HEAT Gently heat a lightly greased 20 cm frypan.

4 Pour batter into a jug for easier pouring.

5 Pour about 3 tablespoons into pan. Tilt pan to spread it all over evenly.

6 Lift edges with a knife. When golden, flip it over and cook the other side.

7 Place on kitchen paper. Sprinkle lemon + sugar over.

8 Roll up and serve hot with whipped cream or ice-cream if you like.

BANANA DELICIOUS

Serves 6

4 medium-sized bananas
1 tablespoon lemon juice
2 eggs
2 tablespoons caster sugar
1 cup desiccated coconut
2 tablespoons apricot jam
cream or ice-cream to
    serve

1 Turn oven to 180°C (350°F) Peel the bananas.

2 Slice the bananas into an ovenproof dish.

3 Sprinkle the lemon juice all over.

4 Put eggs + sugar in bowl. Beat well until creamy.

5 Stir in coconut + jam. Mix it all well.

6 Pour it all evenly over the bananas.

7 Bake for 25 minutes or until golden.

8 Serve warm with cream or ice-cream.

PINEAPPLE CREAM TRIFLE

Serves 6

85 g packet lemon
  jelly crystals
1 cup boiling water
250 g packet jam
  sponge roll
2 tablespoons custard powder

1 cup milk
450 g can crushed
  pineapple, well drained
1¼ cups thickened cream
2 tablespoons icing sugar

Trifles are a great way to use up bits and pieces. Any left-over cake will do as the base; use raspberry jelly and tinned peaches for a different flavour.

1

Put jelly and water in a small bowl. Stir until jelly dissolves.

2

Cut jam roll into slices. Put on bottom of a serving bowl.

3

Pour jelly over cake.

4

Put custard powder and milk in a small pan. Stir until smooth.

5

Cook, stirring slowly, until custard thickens and boils.

6

Take off heat. Stir in pineapple. Put lid on and leave 5 minutes. Spread over jelly.

7

Put cream and sugar in a small bowl. Beat until thick. Spread over custard.

8

Cover bowl with plastic wrap. Put in fridge for 2–3 hours.

MANGO ICE-CREAM

Serves 4

2 teaspoons cornflour
2 tablespoons sugar
1 cup cream
1 cup milk
170 g can mango pulp

1. Mix cornflour, sugar and cream in a pan.

2. Add milk. Cook, stirring, until it boils and thickens.

3. Remove from heat. Leave to cool slightly.

4. Stir in mango pulp.

5. Pour mixture into a big plastic bowl. Cover with plastic wrap.

6. Put in freezer 2 hours until the ice-cream hardens a little.

7. Take out and beat on Medium speed 4 minutes.

8. Put in freezer again for 4 hours or until firm.

APPLE PUDDING

Serves 6

5 green apples
¼ cup caster sugar
1 teaspoon grated lemon
  rind
1 tablespoon water
60 g butter
2 tablespoons caster sugar,
  extra
1 egg
½ cup self-raising flour
cream or ice-cream, to
  serve

1	2	3
 Turn oven to 180°C (350°F) Grease a baking dish.	 Peel, core + slice apples. Put in baking dish.	 Stir in caster sugar + lemon rind. Add the water.

4	5	6
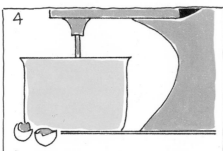 Beat butter, 2 tablespoons sugar + egg till smooth.	 Stir in the flour. Mix well.	Carefully spread it on top of the apples.

7		8
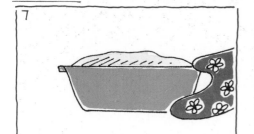 Bake it for 30-35 minutes or until golden.	*You could sprinkle chopped walnuts on top of this pudding before putting it in the oven.*	 Serve warm with cream or vanilla ice-cream.

CREAMY APRICOT RICE

Serves 4

425 g can apricot halves
540 g can vanilla-flavoured
   rice cream
1 teaspoon grated orange
   rind

1¼ cups thickened cream
2 tablespoons icing sugar
2 tablespoons slivered
   almonds, toasted

Think of ways to make the food you cook look great. Serve this dessert in your prettiest glasses.

1
Drain all the liquid from apricots. Chop half of them.

2
Put chopped apricots + rice cream into a big bowl. Add 1 teaspoon rind. Mix gently.

3
Put cream and sugar in a small bowl. Beat until firm peaks form.

4
Put ½ the cream onto the rice. Mix in the rest of the apricots very gently.

5
Spoon into pretty glasses.

6
Put in fridge for 1 hour.

7
Top with the rest of the cream.

8
Sprinkle with almonds. Serve immediately.

CRISPY APRICOT BALLS

Makes 24 balls

⅔ cup crushed plain biscuit crumbs
1 cup Rice Bubbles
⅓ cup desiccated coconut
250 g white chocolate, chopped
1 tablespoon oil
3 tablespoons apricot jam
⅔ cup coloured sprinkles

Roll these balls in crushed nuts or desiccated coconut instead of sprinkles if you like.

1

Put biscuit crumbs, Rice Bubbles and coconut in bowl. Mix gently.

2

Melt chocolate in a bowl over hot water.

3

Take off heat. Add oil. Stir until smooth.

4

Put jam in a small pan. Warm gently – don't let it boil.

5

Make a well in centre of crumb mixture.

6

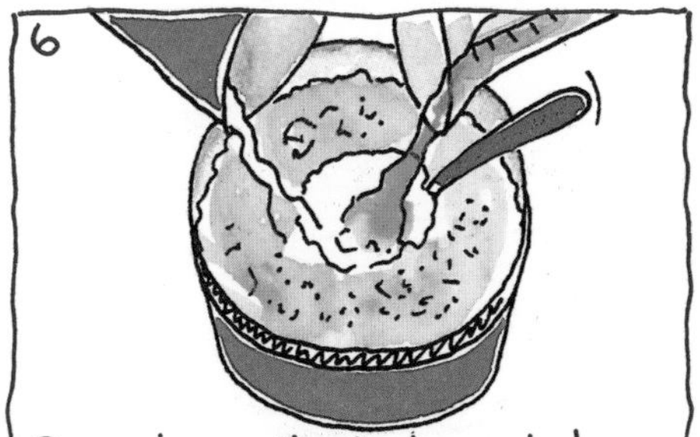

Pour in melted chocolate and jam. Mix gently.

7

Make balls by rolling 1 tablespoon of mixture.

8

Roll balls in sprinkles. Leave to set at room temperature.

FRECKLE FACES

Makes about 12

1 cup self-raising flour
2 tablespoons caster sugar
1 egg, lightly beaten
½ cup milk
1 teaspoon imitation vanilla
  essence
1 teaspoon oil
¼ cup soft cream cheese
¼ cup hazelnut spread
2 tablespoons hundreds
  and thousands

1

Sift flour and sugar into a mixing bowl.

2

Add the egg, milk and vanilla. Beat with a fork until smooth.

3

Brush a non-stick pan with the oil. Put on stove.

4

When pan is hot, put spoonfuls of mixture in about 4 cm apart.

5

Cook for 1 minute, turn, cook other side for 1 minute or until bottom is golden.

6

Leave to cool. Spread half of each pikelet with cheese.

7

Spread other half with hazelnut spread.

Pancake batter can be made one day before you need it. Store in a jug, covered with plastic wrap, in the refrigerator.

8

Sprinkle with hundreds and thousands.

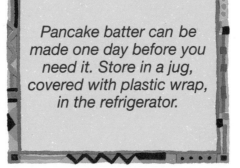

COCONUT MARSHMALLOWS

Makes 16

1 cup sugar
1 tablespoon gelatine
¾ cup hot water
½ teaspoon coconut essence
1 cup desiccated coconut

1
Line a deep 19cm square cake tin with foil.

2
Put sugar, gelatine and water in a small pan. Stir 5 minutes.

3
Simmer 5 minutes more without stirring.

4
Turn up heat. Boil without stirring for 5 minutes more

5
Pour into mixing bowl, leave to cool, then beat for 5 minutes. Stir in essence.

6
Spread marshmallow evenly in tin. Leave for 1 hour until firm.

7
Put coconut in pan. Heat gently until golden. Take off heat and cool.

8
Cut marshmallow in squares and toss in coconut. Wrap brightly.

CHOC-CHERRY SPIDERS

Makes 20
100 g packet glacé cherries
⅓ cup flaked almonds, toasted
100 g packet fried egg noodles
200 g dark chocolate, chopped
30 g butter

1
Chop cherries finely.

2
Put in a bowl with almonds and noodles.

3
Melt chocolate and butter in a small bowl over hot water.

4
Take off heat. Stir until smooth.

5
Add chocolate to cherry mix. Stir gently to combine.

6
Put spoonfuls onto a sheet of greaseproof paper. Leave to set.

7
Dust with icing sugar.

8
Wrap in cellophane and tie with ribbon.

BANANA BITES

Makes about 10

2 medium bananas
125 g milk chocolate melts
1 teaspoon oil
½ cup chocolate sprinkles

1 Peel bananas. Cut off ends.

2 Cut into 3cm slices.

3 Melt chocolate in a bowl over hot water.

4 Take off heat. Add oil. Stir until smooth.

5 Spread sprinkles on a sheet of greaseproof paper.

6 Using a skewer, dip banana into chocolate.

7 Roll banana in sprinkles.

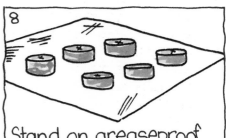

8 Stand on greaseproof paper. Leave to set at room temperature.

Cooking is great fun but before you start, take time to get organised. Read over the recipe thoroughly, read it all the way through and check that you have all the ingredients. Collect everything you need for your recipe — all the ingredients and all the equipment.

If you need to use the oven for baking, turn it on to the correct temperature before you start the recipe. Arrange the oven shelves at the height you want before turning the oven on.

If your recipe calls for chopped or shredded ingredients do this before you begin. Also open any cans and wash any vegetables or fruits. Grease any baking tins if you need to.

All the recipes are set out in easy to follow step-by-step form. Remember to finish each step before beginning the next one.

IMPORTANT SAFETY POINTS

Here are a few hints and tips to make cooking safe and enjoyable.

✔ Always ask an adult for permission before you start.

✔ Before starting to cook, wash your hands well with soap and water. Wear an apron to protect your clothes and wear closed-in, non-slip shoes to protect your feet.

✔ If you have long hair, tie it back so that you don't risk any hairs falling into your cooking. A hair in your lunch or dinner can be a great turnoff to a meal you were finding quite delicious.

✔ Collect everything you need for your recipe before you start – all the ingredients and the necessary kitchen equipment.

✔ Unless you are allowed to use knives, ask an adult to help you chop things. Never cut directly on a kitchen surface – always use a chopping board. When you are using a knife, pick it up by the handle, not by the blade. Keep your fingers well clear of the blade when chopping foods.

✔ Take care when washing knives, too. Keep the sharp edge of the blade away from you and store the knives out of reach of any young brothers or sisters.

✔ Always use oven gloves when you are moving anything into or out of the oven. Remember that anything you take from the oven or from the stove top will stay hot for a while.

✔ Turn saucepan handles to the side when cooking so you don't knock them, and make sure they are not over hotplates that are turned on. Remember to hold the handles of saucepans when stirring foods on the stove and use a wooden spoon or a metal spoon with a wooden handle. (All metal spoons can get hot when stirring foods.)

✔ Place hot saucepans and ovenproof dishes on a chopping board when you take them from the oven or the stove. Never set a hot pan directly on the kitchen bench or table, unless it is covered with ceramic tiles.

✔ When cooking in a microwave, remember to use microwave-safe dishes and containers. Check with an adult if you're not sure.

✔ Some microwave dishes may need stirring during the cooking process to prevent food sticking to the sides and to avoid uneven cooking. You can interrupt the cycle, stir the dish, and press "START" again. Always use oven gloves for microwave cooking because the cooking dish can become very hot.

✔ Be very careful when you remove the plastic wrap that has covered a micowave cooked dish. The steam underneath the plastic can burn your hands.

✔ Never use electrical appliances near water. Always have dry hands before you start to use any appliance.

✔ Be very careful with pots and pans on the stove. Never reach across a hot saucepan of food – steam is very hot and can cause a nasty burn.

✔ Remember to turn off the oven, the hotplate or gas ring or any other appliance when you have finished using it.

✔ Most importantly, clean up the kitchen when you have finished cooking. Put away all the ingredients and the equipment you have used. Wash the dishes – start with washing the least soiled dishes like glassware and bowls and then do the messy pans and baking tins. Dry the dishes thoroughly and put them back in their place. Wipe down your work surface with a clean cloth and then, I'm sure, you'll be allowed to cook again another day.

First Aid for Burns and Scalds

Cool the burnt parts with cold water for at least 10 minutes. Make the hurt person comfortable, but do not move him or her if the burn or scald is serious. Protect against infection by covering the burns or scalds with clean non-adherent material. Do not touch. Do not remove stuck clothing.

If someone's clothing catches fire approach holding a rug, blanket or coat in front of yourself. Wrap it around the person and lay him or her flat. Smother the flames.

If anyone is seriously hurt, ring for an ambulance.

COOK'S TOOLS

There are many tools used in the kitchen to make cooking easy. There are wooden and metal spoons to stir with, spatulas to combine ingredients, bowls of varying sizes to mix things in, strainers or colanders to drain and rinse foods in, and a whole array of different size saucepans and baking trays to cook things in. Then there are wire racks for cooling cakes and cookies, metal spatulas to help you measure and also to spread ingredients or toppings evenly over foods.

The recipes in this book use only basic equipment found in most kitchens. If in doubt about any equipment you may need to ask an adult for some help.

TRICKS OF THE TRADE

SOME SIMPLE COOKING TERMS

BEAT: to stir foods with a spoon or electric mixer until they are smooth.

BOILING POINT: when a liquid bubbles in a steady pattern and the bubbles break on the surface; steam also starts to rise from the pan.

CHOP: to cut food carefully into small pieces. To chop finely is to cut foods as small as you can.

DRAIN: to strain away unwanted liquid using a colander or strainer, as when you have cooked spaghetti. Do this over the kitchen sink so that water can drain away down the sink. Ask an adult for help, as a large pan of water can be very heavy.

GRATE: to rub food against a grater. Do this over kitchen paper. Hold the grater with one hand and rub the food back and forth over the grating holes. This gives you long thin pieces. For finely grated foods use the smallest grating holes.

GREASE: to rub baking tins and cooking utensils with butter, margarine or oil to stop foods sticking when you bake them.

MASH: to squash cooked or very ripe foods with a fork or potato masher.

SEPARATING EGGS: for making use of egg whites or yolks. Hold the egg over a small plate and carefully crack the shell with a metal spatula or table knife. Let the egg fall out onto the plate, place a small glass over the yolk and then carefully tip the white into a bowl. If any yolk gets into the white, you can easily remove it with a piece of eggshell.

SIMMER: to cook food over a very low heat so that only a few bubbles appear over the surface. When a recipe calls for food to boil and then simmer, simply turn the heat down to the lowest setting.

SLICE: to cut foods like apples, carrots and tomatoes into thin rounds or sections.

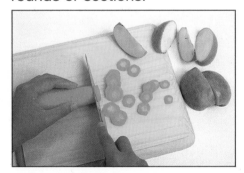

STIR: to combine ingredients by stirring them together in a bowl or saucepan.

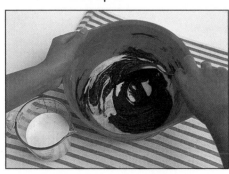

COOKED INGREDIENTS

Some of the recipes in this book call for cooked rice, pasta, vegetables and mashed vegetables. If you don't have any of these cooked foods as leftovers in your refrigerator you will need to prepare them before you start your recipe. Follow these guidelines and if in doubt ask for adult help.

TO COOK RICE AND PASTA

Firstly you will need to put a large saucepan of water on to boil. (Use 2 L water for 500 g pasta.) Add 1 tablespoon of oil to the water. For 2½ cups of cooked rice or pasta you will need 1 cup uncooked rice or pasta. Add the rice or pasta to the steadily boiling water, stir in carefully and cook for 8–12 minutes or until tender. You may need to ask an adult to help you drain it in a colander or strainer over the sink because a large pot of water can be very heavy. Use the rice or pasta immediately for hot dishes or rinse well with cold water and cool for cold dishes.

Add oil to boiling water.

Add pasta to boiling water; stir.

TO COOK VEGETABLES

Wash vegetables, trim if necessary and cut into required shape. Put a large saucepan of water on to boil, and when boiling very carefully lower vegetables into water. Cook until vegetables are just tender. If in doubt ask an adult to help you test your vegetables for doneness, and then ask them to assist you with draining them.

For mashed potatoes or pumpkin it is best to cook them a little longer until soft and then drain them. Place them in a bowl and use a potato masher or fork to squash them to a mushy consistency.

Cut into even-sized pieces.

Drain vegetables using a colander.

Mash with a vegetable masher.

GLOSSARY

Australian	British	American
beetroot	beetroot	beet
bicarbonate of soda	bicarbonate of soda	baking soda
biscuit	biscuit	cookie
biscuit tray	baking sheet	cookie sheet
blender	liquidizer	blender
cake tin	cake tin	cake pan
capsicum	sweet pepper	bell pepper
caster sugar	caster sugar	superfine sugar
cling wrap	polythene wrap	plastic wrap
cornflour	cornflour	cornstarch
devon	bologna	bologna
eggplant	aubergine	eggplant
fish fingers	fish fingers	fish sticks
flour		
plain	plain	all-purpose
self-raising	self-raising	self-rising
frankfurt	frankfurter	frankfurter
glacé fruit	glace fruit	candied fruit
golden syrup	golden syrup	light corn syrup
grill	grill	broil
hundreds and thousands	nonpareils	nonpareils
icing sugar	icing sugar	confectioners' sugar
lemonade	carbonated lemonade	Seven Up or Sprite
cream		
single	single	light
thickened	double	heavy
lolly	sweet	candy
Morning Coffee biscuits	flat sweet biscuits	flat sweet cookies
oven tray	baking sheet	cookie sheet
pan	frying pan	skillet
pie dish	pie dish	pie pan
pikelet	pikelet	small pancake
pitta	pitta	pita
prawn	prawn	shrimp
Rice Bubbles	Rice Krispies	Rice Krispies
scone	scone	biscuit
snow pea	mange tout	snow pea
spring onions	spring onions	scallions
tomato sauce	tomato sauce	tomato ketchup
Vegemite	Marmite	yeast or vegetable extract
zucchini	courgettes	zucchini

INDEX

Published by Murdoch Books®, a division of Murdoch Magazines Pty Limited,
213 Miller Street, North Sydney NSW 2060
Murdoch Books® Associate Food Editors: Kerrie Ray and Tracy Rutherford
Authors: Mary Pat Fergus, Rosalie Higson
Photography: Ray Joyce, Andrew Furlong, Jon Bader
Art Direction and Design: Wing Ping Tong, Jan Gosewinckel, Jayne Hunter
Illustrations: Mary Pat Fergus, Jayne Hunter
Recipe Development: Voula Mantzouridis
Food Stylists: Janice Baker, Georgina Dolling, Marie Hélène Clauzon
Food Stylists' Assistant: Jodie Vassallo
Border Artwork: Jan Gosewinckel

Publisher: Anne Wilson
Publishing Manager: Catie Ziller
Managing Editor: Susan Tomnay
Studio Manager: Norman Baptista
International Manager: Mark Newman
Marketing Manager: Mark Smith
National Sales Manager: Keith Watson
Photo Librarian: Dianne Bedford

Canadian Cataloguing-in-Publication Data
Best of kids' cooking
Includes index.
ISBN 1 55110 391 5
1. Cookery – Juvenile literature
TX652.5.B47 1995 j641.5'123 C95-910811-4

First printed 1994. This edition 1995.

Produced by Mandarin Offset, Hong Kong

Distributed in Canada by Whitecap Books Ltd,
351 Lynn Avenue, North Vancouver, British Columbia, V7J 2C4